This is the story of Megan Rose who was abducted twice by malevolent extraterrestrials and rescued by benevolent Nordic aliens. She kept in touch with her rescuer and has brought in this book, the story of a galactic war on planet Earth, as explained by her Nordic friends from the stars. The people of Earth have falsely been led to believe that aliens don't exist. The knowledge of extraterrestrial life in this solar system is imperative to the understanding of Earth's past, present and future. Through the awakening of humanity to the existence of extraterrestrial life, a new era is birthed for all inhabitants of the planet and this galaxy. Welcome to the Future.

WELCOME TO THE FUTURE

An Alien abduction, A Galactic War and the Birth of a New Era

Megan Rose

ISBN 9798756237467

Author's Website: *meganrosemedium.com*

YouTube: *Megan Rose*

About the Author: Megan Rose was born and raised in Northern Virginia, in the suburbs of Washington, D.C. She graduated college with a nursing degree from State College of Florida. Her passion for taking care of others led her to a career in the intensive care unit at a hospital in South Florida. As she awakened to her true nature, Megan started her own business as a psychic medium and soon left the hospital for another adventure. Her commitment to healing transcends any job title, as she delivers her work with the greatest love.

It is my greatest honor to dedicate this book

to all the children of planet Earth

who have been tortured, raped, abused and murdered

at the hands of the dark forces.

May your souls feel the freedom of Victory

as we rise together as Champions of the Galaxy.

Megan Rose

Acknowledgements:

My deepest gratitude to my protector in the stars, Val Nek Artovea, for without his dedication to humanity and myself, this book would not be possible. His love and protection in this lifetime and the next have been the greatest gift. To the crew who rescued me, Thor Han and Celadion, their bravery and love for justice is uncanny. Myrah for her love and comfort during my hardest times as a child. High Commander Ardaana, for seeing the battle through and leading my galactic friends. Anelsa, your love and kindness make my heart soar with pride. Raydeon, for his smile has never failed to melt my heart into pieces. Thank you to my mom, dad, and siblings for loving me no matter what. And lastly, thank you to the bullies of my life, alien and human, for without you, I may have never found the courage within myself to accept the challenge of this mission.

Megan Rose's contacts with Val Nek from the Galactic Federation of Worlds have been truly remarkable for the scope and breadth of the information that has been released. Val Nek's updates are eagerly anticipated all over the world by many thousands eager to learn the truth about a Galactic War where Earth has played an outsized role. Megan's life story, psychic skills, and extraterrestrial contacts are described in detail in this, her first book, and make for exceptional reading. Most importantly, this book will help awaken you to how you can help usher in a New Era for humanity.

Michael Salla, Ph.D.

An Abduction of a Star Child

A Star Baby

From the time I was little, I was looked after by the people of the stars. Not known to Earth, for no one knew they existed, I was loved and cared for by extraterrestrial life, flying in ships in the distant sky. The people of this planet were fooled into believing that extraterrestrial life did not exist. I was born onto a planet where people did not believe in me, or the world I came from. So began the mission to bring to this world what no one expected: knowledge of Earth's star neighbors.

When I was a toddler, I remember lying in my crib and watching glowing orbs of light dance above me, sending me feelings of love and the comfort of home. While suddenly, a flash of light was emitted from the doorway. I found myself floating up, up and away. I was just a toddler, with a full head of brown hair and red chubby cheeks. Curiously, my surroundings had changed from my bedroom to what appeared to be an alien ship. Standing in front of me was a tall brown-skinned alien with a large bald head and indigo eyes. Next to him was a tall blonde-haired, blue-eyed woman with large, wide set eyes. I would later learn that her name was Anelsa. She was from a planet called Erra, in the Ashaara system, what we on Earth call Taygeta in the Pleiades star cluster. This woman spoke to me in a methodical language, and I was soon put to sleep by her cold touch on my forehead. A process that is commonly done to erase memory. Far into the future, I would be allowed to remember again. This incident was a medical check-up, a benevolent abduction by my protectors in the stars.

The First Abduction

A normal little girl, I enjoyed playing with my dolls and watching Barney on the television. Growing up in the suburbs of Washington D.C., life as a little kid was quite simple and I had all of the treasures that marked an ordinary childhood. Bike riding, swinging, and playing with the other kids in the neighborhood, were all things I enjoyed.

I was only five years old when one night while asleep in my bedroom, a flash of light appeared next to my bed. Three small grey aliens surrounded my bed. They had small mouths and only four fingers on each hand. They were making humming and clicking noises, as if communicating with each other. To my horror, I was paralyzed and taken aboard a triangular shaped craft. They stripped me naked and began preparing for some sort of operation on a cold table. I couldn't move, but I could feel the tears in my eyes well up as I looked above me and saw a tall, grey alien with a long face and large eyes. He smelled terrible, like rotten eggs, and I could feel his curiosity in me growing as he took his long, bony finger and ran it down my face. I could not tell if I was too scared to move or if I was truly paralyzed. The tall grey made his way to the top of my bed, standing behind my head. Next to him was a shorter grey and he was instructing to him directions. The small grey had an instrument in his hand that emitted a red light, like a laser pointer. I learned later that this device allowed them to see through the layers of my brain. The tall grey was from the race Maytra, and they were known for placing tracking devices in the cerebral cortex of their victims. They abduct women and children for genetic experiments and hybridization, and they commonly place tracking devices to locate the humans they experimented on. As the small grey peered into my brain, the tall Maytra became extremely angry, starting to spit as he made strange noises, his breath smelling terrible. A feeling of anger pervaded the room and it became clear the Maytra was upset at what he saw. Unbeknownst to me, I had a special implant placed as a baby. A different type of advanced technology that was used by my star protectors, members of the Galactic Federation of Worlds. The implant monitored by brainwaves, ensuring my brain would develop normally and was placed for my protection.

The Maytra

Seconds later, the entire ship rocked, and I heard loud screeching sounds along with men's voices shouting. Flashes of light occurred as the door to this cold room burst open. A tall man wearing a bluish-silver super suit and helmet entered with a few others in tow, all wearing the same outfit. The first man I would later come to know and remember as Val Nek Artovaya, a pilot from the Galactic Federation of Worlds. Val Nek pointed his laser gun at the Maytra's head, and it screeched as it completely collapsed to the ground. The pilot ran to my side and scooped me up as the rest of his crew inflicted death upon the tall grey's minion workers.

I was taken aboard my rescuer's ship, a much different environment and familiar to me in many ways, although I could not quite articulate why. While sitting on a seat near the back of the ship, I could see to the left of me a control panel and two chairs. There were blond men sitting in the chairs and I realized the craft was moving at an undetermined speed. Tears were streaming from my face as I was still confused from the events of the night. My rescuer, Val Nek, kneeled in front of me, wiping my tears. Right behind him was a blonde humanoid woman with cat-like features. I was wrapped in a soft fabric, material I had never quite felt before. The blonde woman, whose name was Myrah, gently took my hand, I could feel her touch, it was as soft as silk. She looked me over, as if inspecting me and nodded to Val Nek, reassuring him of my safety.

Val Nek had removed his helmet, his wispy blond hair falling over his eyebrows. He had a piercing gaze, dark blue indigo eyes and glowing pale skin. He was incredibly handsome with prominent cheekbones and a strong jawline. As a little girl I had learned of angels and I thought for certain that he must be one of them. I had a deep love for him, as if I had known him my whole life and longer. Before he erased my memory with his cold hand to my forehead, he said this:

> "I am very sorry that this happened to you, my dear girl. We will never let it happen again. You are mine to protect and I will be watching over you, for the rest of your life, and for much longer after that. You and I are bonded through love and I am never far away. I will erase your memory of this moment, but one day it will be time to remember."

Val Nek

The Second Abduction

When I was nine years old, the monsters were back again. The little greys appeared in my bedroom with a flash of light. Instantly, I seemed to be paralyzed, unable to move or scream. All I wanted to do was run and scream. I was taken to a large cylinder ship that was floating above my cul-de-sac in the suburbs of Northern Virginia. The next thing I remember, I was lying flat on a table with extremely bright lights over me. My head was heavy, I could not lift it and my entire body was pins and needles. Breathing over me was a tall, reptile-like being. He was covered in scales. The first thing I noticed about him was his nose. He just had two slanted slits that he was breathing out of. He was breathing rather heavily, grunting even, as he was thinking. I got the impression he was in charge of what was happening. He had his large, muscular arms crossed, folded over his chest. There was no compassion in his eyes, he had vertical slits for pupils, which were full of hatred for me. This reptilian species is known for their psychic abilities. They can invade the minds of their prey and often enjoy projecting fear into the consciousness of their victim. To my horror, I was sharing a telepathic connection with this being. I could read his thoughts and he could read mine. Through this method, I came to understand how I got here. The reptilian soldier had been watching me for a while. I was part of his "list". I did not know what that meant at the time, but Val Nek, my rescuer, later explained that each person's DNA has an energetic frequency. This frequency can be tracked down using technology from a higher density. He explained that this is how they track down and identify certain children or people that would be useful to them. The reptilian was aware of my DNA and was interested in using me for several different things. Because of my aptitude for certain psychic abilities, he had plans to take me through a portal to Mars to be a slave and super soldier.

The term "super soldier" is used to describe a person, often taken against their will, who is trained to be part of a secret space program. Many of these secret space programs use trauma-based mind control where they "split" the mind and program different alters to do different missions.

My potential for psychic abilities, such as telekinesis, would make me a useful asset if they were successful in traumatizing me enough to transform me into a weapon. The reptilian also was interested in putting me in breeding programs and harvesting my eggs. I began to understand that he was instructing the small greys to perform a procedure that would violate me, in order to harvest my eggs and make hybrid children. One of the small greys grabbed my arm and a milky white substance started running into my veins. The air on the ship was already thin, but it was even harder to breathe as the substance caused my muscles to be paralyzed even further and my entire body became numb. I started to feel like I was dying.

If someone consents to an abduction, then they cannot be rescued. Often these malevolent extraterrestrials use fear to gain consent for procedures or abductions. The reptilian told me if I didn't agree to go with him, he would kill my mother. He had invaded my mind and was telepathically bullying me. He sent images of my mother being chopped up in pieces into my mind. He said if I didn't let him take me, my whole family, including my young siblings, would be killed. As a child who had many nightmares and terrors, I always reminded myself, even in dream state, that monsters aren't real. I continued to say, "no, you're not real", and the gigantic reptilian grew angrier.

All of a sudden, the reptilian's mind shifted from hatred and malice to a feeling of trepidation. I telepathically was linked to the reptilian and I understood that he felt he had made a mistake. He had overlooked something. His eyes started to dart back and forth, and for the first time, words came out of his mouth. They were not English words; they were forceful and sounded like a hissing. The ship started to rock, and I could hear men's voices shouting in the background. The door to the room burst open, just as it did in my first abduction. My friends were here! I recognized Val Nek, my rescuer from my first abduction, as he grabbed the reptilian by the neck. Val Nek later explained to me that there are access points, certain spots underneath the neck of this reptilian species where they are particularly sensitive. While it's not ideal to inflict harm this way, as it is much easier to shoot them with laser guns, Val Nek's anger inspired him to kill the reptilian with his bare hands. I had never seen him so angry; he gripped the reptilian's neck with his thumb and forefinger, thrusting with force.

The Reptilian

Blood started to spill from the reptilians neck and eyes, and as it splashed onto his super suit, it dissolved and evaporated instantly. The reptilian fell to the ground and another member of the crew shot him with a laser gun. Val Nek, dressed in a bluish-silver super suit and a helmet, scooped me up in his arms and took me back to his ship.

Val Nek was concerned for my health and wanted me to be checked by medical personnel of the Galactic Federation as soon as possible. I could hear his heart beating fast as he placed me down on a table and took off his helmet. His familiar face appeared from underneath the bluish-silver helmet, his blond hair falling slightly over his eyebrows, which were furrowed in anger. He stood next to me as I lay on the table, his arms folded and his chest puffed out. He was quite tall and muscular, with a commanding presence. I recognized the rest of the crew, now that their helmets were removed. Another tall man with wavy blond shoulder length hair was present, a pilot named Thor Han. On the other side of me were two beautiful women with blond hair, my friends Anelsa and Myrah. Both women were medical personnel from the Federation. Val Nek's dark blue eyes were watching their every move as they inspected me for any signs of harm. His protective instincts were in overdrive, and he did not want to let they or anyone else touch me, although he knew this was in my best interest. To Val Nek's relief, my physical trauma was healed by Myrah, but I was still mentally traumatized by the torture I was subjected to by the reptilian warrior.

My tears were stifled as my friends quickly made attempts to lighten the mood. Val Nek put his hand on my shoulder and escorted me to a round table with seating, like a booth at a restaurant. The table was also a holographic scene, a map of the solar system. He winked at me, motioning to the holographic images and said, "Go ahead, you will like this." I began playing, finding it fascinating how the screen on the table moved as you touched it. It was amazing technology that is not found on Earth, at least not yet. Nearing the time for my return, I sat to the right of Val Nek as he drove the ship back to Earth to take me home. My eyes grew wide as we flew past the moon. I had never seen it that close before, it was bright white and other spaceships were flying near it.

We came to hover over my cul-de-sac and although I had had a terrible night, I longed to remain in Val Nek's protective presence. I could feel his relief as my safe return home was successful, thanks to him and his crew from the Galactic Federation. He kneeled down at my eye level and gave me a hug. He spoke very softly and said, "This night is something that should have never happened. I am very sorry this could not have been prevented. I will continue to watch over you, it is my greatest honor and duty. Our bond is stronger than the distant memories of this night. I will have to erase your memory, for your protection, so you can live a normal life. You have nothing to fear, for our bond of love is stronger than our worst day." He took his hand and touched my forehead. I suddenly became dizzy and fell to sleep.

Home Is Where the Heart Is: Implant Placement

I continued to grow up and live a normal life, never fully remembering the nightly adventures of my childhood, but I always had a deep knowing that I was loved and protected. The trauma of my abductions manifested itself into a variety of phobias. I was afraid to fall asleep, go to the doctor's office for a checkup, and I also always slept with all my limbs under a blanket, for fear something would grab me. I had distant memories of shadow figures standing over me but could never place the exact experience.

By September 2019, I had graduated college and was working as a registered nurse in the intensive care unit of a local hospital in south Florida. One evening, I was sound asleep when a bright white-bluish light beamed over me, and I was taken aboard a ship belonging to the Galactic Federation of Worlds. Standing in front of me was a tall, athletic blond man. His dark blue eyes were beaming with joy and unconditional love filled my heart. I ran to hug him, my guardian angel from the sky. Val Nek is from Epsilon Eridani, a planet that was colonized by Nordic aliens from the Ashaara or Taygeta system in the Pleiades. He whispered in my ear, "I have a surprise for you!"

Val Nek stepped aside and standing behind him was a younger blond man with similar facial features as Val Nek, a strong jawline and high cheekbones, except he had larger, bright blue eyes. The man was also beaming with joy, he nodded his head and said, "Hello there", with a smile. Tears welled up in my eyes as I ran to hug him. His name was Raydeon and he was also from a planet named Erra, in the Pleiades. Joy filled my heart as the soul connection I had to these two men overwhelmed me. I was home.

The two men flew me to a larger ship, a mothership, it was a science lab for the Galactic Federation of Worlds. Once aboard the ship, Val Nek took my hand and escorted me down the long corridor. The hallway had a beautiful view, large windows (later I would learn that these are not windows, but technology that allows viewing to the outside) as walls. I became slightly afraid and squeezed Val Nek's hand, I had always been afraid of heights and was keenly aware that we were floating in the sky. Val Nek laughed as we came to two white double doors and entered an auditorium. As we entered, I noticed the familiar face of Myrah, walking towards us with her arms open, she motioned to give me a hug. Myrah is a medical scientist and implant specialist. She takes care of the rescued hybrid children, among other tasks for the Galactic Federation. Myrah smiled as she pointed to Val Nek, teasing him, "Did he tell you why he brought you here?" As a matter of fact, I thought, he didn't. I was so overwhelmed with joy to see Val Nek and Raydeon, that I didn't bother asking where or what we were doing. Val Nek spoke, "As part of your mission, Myrah is going to upgrade your implant to a high grade communication device. Things on planet Earth are heating up, and I need you to be able to communicate with me, whenever needed. I will teach you how to use it over the next several months." I agreed without reservation, Val Nek has always protected me, and I trusted them both. Myrah motioned for me to sit down and with her expertise, placed an implant for communication in my head. This procedure was done in a different density and the implant placed looked like a frequency that held a disk shape. It was not solid matter and was tuned to the fifth density, the frequency of the Galactic Federation. The federation uses this technology on military personnel for communication, but also to pilot a ship. The pilots of the federation merge their consciousness via the implant to the consciousness of the ship.

The implant placed was the same technology and not hackable by the enemy. I heard different high-pitched frequencies until suddenly, I heard a "POP" noise. Pleased with her work, Myrah smiled. I could hear them even clearer in my head, their voices much louder and now with an echo.

Myrah escorted me around the lab, giving me a tour of the facility. She explained that she was working on healing the rescued hybrid children from the deep underground military bases on Earth. There were small children, who looked to be about ages nine to eleven in vertical pods. Myrah brought me to one of the pods containing a young boy, around age nine. His skin was a bluish-grey color and I could see his veins running through his body. He was bald and his facial features were not those of a normal human. He had a small nose, almost slits, and a very small mouth. "This is a hybrid child from planet Terra, he contains a reptiloid and human genome. These poor children have never known love and he has never seen the light of day. He was born into captivity and has been kept in a stasis pod his whole life. This child has been a project of mine, he was created for a special purpose, and has rare genetics, even more rare than the other hybrids. We are unsure if he will be able to survive outside of the pod. It is a long tiring process, but I will not give up hope", Myrah said with a serious look on her face. She turned to me and smiled, her eyes getting bigger, "Now, I will show you our greatest success." We walked down the corridor to a room full of children playing. Myrah beamed as she explained these were the rescued children who were socializing. They had made a complete recovery and were waiting to be transported to new homes around the solar system. I noticed two little blue children, a boy and a girl, with no hair and bright green eyes playing tag. I stared at them, thinking how beautiful they were, and the joy they expressed was magnificent. Myrah winked at me and said, "I know." Val Nek approached us, signaling to me, it was time for me to return home.

Aboard the smaller space craft and nearing my house once again, I became increasingly upset about my return to planet Earth. I begged him to let me stay with him and the rest of my star friends. Before beaming me down, Val Nek sighed and said this: "Your mission is not over and in fact, has only just begun. I am very sorry, but you must go back to complete your work.

I will always be here for you and now you will be able to communicate with me, whenever you want or need. I will be teaching you things about your planet, and I need you to be strong and use your voice. Do not be afraid and do not consent to fear."

In the following months, my memories of my childhood abductions and who I truly was returned to me. My psychic abilities were turned on like a light switch, especially my clairvoyance. It became increasingly apparent, and although I loved my job as a registered nurse, the hospital was not the place for me any longer. I left my job as a nurse and began my work to bring peace and love from the stars to the people of Terra (more commonly known as planet Earth).

The Starseed Envoy Program

The numbers of these envoys may be less than expected as it is not a common occurrence in relation to the number of people on planet Terra. These envoys, the care of their vessels and protection, while on Terra requires a vast number of resources from the Galactic Federation of Worlds as well as the Council of Five. The purpose of the envoy program is to bring extraterrestrial knowledge and technology to the people of Terra. The envoys are extraterrestrials who resonate at a higher density, fifth density and above. Once incarnated into the third density, the envoy forgets its previous incarnation to blend in with the local people, but always knowing on a deep level that they came to bring the knowledge of their home planet to Earth.

To become an envoy, it is a contract of work through the Galactic Federation. The Federation works alongside the Council of Five, whom are masters of genetics, to create vessels for members of the Federation to incarnate here on Terra.

This is advanced technology, not known to the Terran people. The envoy incarnates for a specific mission on Terra, a life purpose, perhaps, but a specific mission. Not every envoy is successful as this is a war zone and the spiritual implications and stress of the incarnation can distract and dismantle the envoy's mission.

The genetics of these envoys is a delicate task. The envoy will choose to leave its original physical vessel in its alien home (alien to Terra) and enter a new physical vessel with their light body (soul). This physical vessel is prepared by the Galactic Federation of Worlds, but also the Council of Five. The Council of Five monitors the evolution, the genomes in Terra, and assists with the evolution of the human race by conducting benevolent abductions. They use their technology to modify the genomes on the mother's side of the family. For on the X chromosome, the genome will be handed down to the subsequent generations. In some cases, they also add additional genomes that are specific to the envoy's mission. For example, if part of the envoy's mission was to become a genetic researcher and bring information from their home planet to Terra, the genome that carried that information would be incorporated into the human vessel, for cellular memory. At some point in the incarnation, this memory would appear as either subconscious or conscious, depending on the spiritual evolution in this incarnation. Spiritual evolution is important to success of the starseed envoy mission in terms of frequency. As the traumas of the human lifetime are transmuted and transcended, the frequency of the light body is increased, which then activates the genomes from the home planet that carry the genetic encoding for the mission. Quite simply, raising the soul frequency activates the DNA and activates the envoy for the mission on Terra.

The original physical vessels on the home alien planet of the envoy are kept in what is called stasis pods. They are vertical pods, most of the time. They are powered by source energy. Source energy also surrounds the physical vessel while in the pod, contained into microscopic crystalline structures infused in a gel like substance, some would call "life support". The physical vessel has an auric field, a small one, that is enforced and nurtured by source. In a normal physical vessel that is inhabited by a light body, the health of the body is also maintained by connecting to source. Since these vessels in stasis pods do not have light bodies that connect to source, it is necessary that they are maintained using source energy for maximum preservation. The vessels in stasis pods, are looked after by scientists of the federation. The federation encompasses a large amount of Ahel scientists, a race from the planet Erra, which is in the star system that humans call the Pleiades. They are often referred to as Nordic aliens.

When time to leave the alien physical vessel for the mission, this is done with the Council of Five present. The light body is escorted through a portal to the human mother's womb, where the light body is instructed to enter. When the mission is over, the reverse process takes place. The soul or light body is either escorted when natural death of the human vessel occurs or in more rare cases, the human vessel is taken aboard a ship of the Federation and is escorted home. This occasion is rare and depends on the terms and conditions of the contract signed with the Federation before the incarnation.

Extra-Terran Soul Matrix: The envoys have what is called an extra-terran soul matrix. The light body of the envoys is of a different structure of light. If you can imagine sacred geometry, the light body is of a different matrix than a terrestrial soul known to planet Terra. Because the soul matrix has a different light structure, it emits a different frequency unknown to Terra. This is also the reason for the genetic modification of the human vessel. The physical Terran vessel must be able to carry the frequency of an extra-Terran soul matrix. The genetics are modified and extraterrestrial DNA is added so that the frequency and structure of the light body can be accommodated by the human physical vessel.

Future Proves Past: A Galactic War

The Invasion

Planet Earth, or Terra, was invaded by two malevolent extraterrestrial groups known to this galaxy between the 1940s-1950s:

The Orion Alliance or The Nebu

A group from the Orion star system comprised of six different races of grey aliens. All races are aggressive extraterrestrials with a need for conquest of power and domination. Races include: Maytra (tall greys) and Killy Tokurt (tall whites).

The Ciakahrr Empire

This group is what Terran people refer to as reptilians but are also referred to as the Ciakahrr Empire. They come from the constellation Alpha Draconis and are sometimes referred to as Draconians. They are tall, muscular, reptile like beings. They have a large military in search for conquest and power in this solar system.

Planet Terra had been visited by extraterrestrial life for eons. However, an invasion of malevolent extraterrestrial species from the Orion and Alpha Draconis systems would prove to be one of humanity's most significant visitations. The German-Nazis formed an alliance with an aggressive extraterrestrial species from Alpha Draconis called the Ciakahrr Empire, or more commonly known to the Terran people as Reptilians. This alliance is also known as the Dark Fleet. The Reptilians promised the Nazis space travel in exchange for Terran resources and underground facilities. The origin of these agreements is near the end of World War II.

In the United States, President Eisenhower's administration signed secret agreements with the Orion Greys behind his back. This is referred to as the Greada Treaty, signed in 1954 by Eisenhower's military industrial complex, often referred to as the Majestic 12 or MJ-12. The betrayal of the Eisenhower administration, and the rectification of these events started a planetary war on the moon, Mars and planet Earth.

As part of the agreements, these extraterrestrials would be allotted facilities on Planet Terra. These facilities were mostly underground and are referred to as deep underground military bases. The Orion group and Ciakahrr Empire were also promised humans to experiment on. The ethics of their operations dwindled over time and soon the Terran government leaders were secretly allowing a large amount of humans to be trafficked to the reptilian and Orion alliance, which resulted in a global human trafficking ring. These humans were either sold or abducted for various purposes. The Orion Alliance and the Ciakahrr Empire participated in genetic experiments and slave trade of humans.

The most egregious of these crimes was supplying adults, children and babies to the reptilian empire for food supply. The slave trade of humans benefited their military factions. Humans were forced to be soldiers and taken against their will to Mars, the moon, Antarctica and underground military bases. The cabal on Terra became deeply involved with the extraterrestrial invaders and the governments of Terra became submissive to their demands.

In the beginning, the benefit of the government leaders to agree to the Orion Greys and Reptilians terms was an exchange of technology. This technology included space craft and other technological "advances" that turned out to be less than fruitful. The government leaders of Terra were fooled into being invaded. The malevolent extraterrestrials acquired land and resources on a foreign planet, with full permission of the inhabiting species. The technology traded to the human government was laughable, just enough to placate them until they required more help from the new invaders.

This required the government of Terra to increasingly become more dependent on them over the years, until the government of Earth was run by the malevolent extraterrestrial species.

The Cabal

Referred to as "black hats", the term cabal is used to describe the Terran leaders who work alongside the Orion Alliance and Ciakahrr Empire for demise and domination of humanity.

The Intervention

The invasion of Terra, Terra's moon, and Mars posed a substantial threat to the rest of the galaxy. Without intervention, the malevolent extraterrestrial conquest of these planets would result in a massive empire of darkness that would threaten life inhabiting the entire galaxy. This negative timeline was foreseen by the Andromeda Council, which requested the Galactic Federation of Worlds to intervene and secure a positive future timeline for the rest of the galaxy.

The Galactic Federation of Worlds and the Council of Five contacted Terran governments in the 1950's with the intention of persuading government leaders to form an alliance with the Galactic Federation of Worlds. The government leaders, including Eisenhower's cabinet, were not impressed with the Federation's disdain for nuclear weapons. One of the requirements for an alliance with the Federation was the dismantling of nuclear bombs. Unimpressed with the Federation's offer, agreements with the Orion Group were instead signed in the Greada Treaty of 1954. Unlike his cabinet members and military industrial complex, President Eisenhower was intrigued by the Galactic Federation of Worlds. He befriended one of their representatives, Valiant Thor, or Val Thor. Val Thor was sent by the Federation to offer the Terran leaders a different future, one that would promise hope for the people of Terra.

The Galactic Federation of Worlds began working with certain factions of Terran military, specifically, the United States Navy, to prepare the planet for the future to come.

The Galactic Federation of Worlds

The Galactic Federation of Worlds is a benevolent galactic military comprised of many different races from many different planets pledged to work for peace and balance in this solar system. A large amount of their military is comprised of Nordic extraterrestrials and humanoid beings. They are governed by a body of laws, called the Prime Directive. They have a law of non-intervention; they do not interfere with a developing society like Planet Terra. However, in the interest of balance and accordance with the Prime Directive, they have a duty to intervene if a developing society has been invaded by a regressive extraterrestrial species such as the Orion Alliance or Ciakahrr Empire.

The Andromeda Council

One of the most spiritually evolved groups of benevolent extraterrestrials is the Andromeda Council or Council of Zenae. They are from the Andromeda Galaxy and are humanoid beings with blue skin. They possess technology that can see far into the future and predict future timelines. They foresaw the fate of this galaxy and requested the military presence in this solar system, the Galactic Federation of Worlds, to intervene.

The Council of Five

A benevolent group of five races, also referred to as the Orion Council of Light or the Council of Five. This group performs positive abductions and assists humanity in the starseed envoy program.

They work alongside the Galactic Federation of Worlds and assist in spiritual evolution. The Council was originally formed to counteract the dark forces of the Orion Greys or Orion Alliance.

The Earth Alliance

Commonly referred to as "white hats", the Earth Alliance consists of Terran leaders committed to fighting the cabal and are partnered with the Galactic Federation of Worlds.

The Q Movement

The Q Movement was a United States naval intelligence operation that emerged on the internet of Terra during the Trump Administration. Many Terrans observed this operation as the work of the Trump Administration, however, it was the work of the Earth Alliance and the United States Navy. The purpose of the operation was not to secure President Trump a second term, but a highly important operation with extraterrestrial involvement.

The US Navy operated this program from secure naval intelligence servers, a simple fact that the mainstream media conveniently ignored. The movement encouraged patriotism and family. It was the Federation and the Earth Alliance's goal, to reveal certain truths regarding the cabal on planet Terra. The operation revealed the existence of elite pedophile and human trafficking rings that were serving the extraterrestrial infiltration on Terra. As popularity of this movement grew, so did the counterintelligence operations. The counterintelligence discredited the movement in the following ways: they refuted the Q movement as a conspiracy on the mainstream media and secondly, spread lies and confusion among the followers of the movement via the internet. The operation was successful, although many Americans felt disappointed in the presidential election of 2020, it was all part of the plan. Future proves past.

September 14, 2021

Val Nek connected with me on this date to reveal the data transcribed below:

<u>VN:</u> It is now time to reveal what will prove to be one of the most important movements in human history: the movement the Terran people call Q. As I have previously confirmed that the Galactic Federation of Worlds has been in contact with the US Navy, it is together, with technology from the Galactic Federation, in the interest of balance, and to counteract the mind control narrative of the Dark Fleet, the Nebu, and the Ciakahrr Empire that we assisted in creating this movement. This program includes US Naval Intelligence along with the alliance and Federation.

Our technology, which was used in this case, to assist in moving the human race onto the ideal timeline, the timeline in which the planet Terra become members of the Federation and are liberated from control of these nefarious influences. Future proves past. We used this movement to prove our intel using data and facts. Combined with our quantum technology, the movement, in many respects, was successful, as we are now transitioning into the reality, we have strived so hard for.

The technology, I can explain, is used by the Andromeda Council. This Council, as some of you know, predicted the fate of this galaxy, far into the future, to be unfavorable for all members of the Federation, planet Terra and the entire Solar System. It was the Council of Zenae who gave us permission to use their timeline technology to intervene, in the interest of balance, with the Terran people. This technology uses mathematical equations that are not known to Earth. The mathematical sequences are formulated and used to trace energy signatures throughout space and time. By doing so, it pinpoints certain events in the time space continuum.

These events are extracted and can be re-arranged to form a positive or negative timeline. So, the Federation, in partnershiphip with the Andromeda Council, extracted dates and times, re-arranged them using mathematical equations to create a timeline that benefits the entire galaxy. Welcome to the future.

The Covid-19 Vaccine

The Covid-19 virus is a genetically modified virus that was created in the Wuhan lab and funded unknowingly by the Terran people. In partnership with the Nebu or Orion Alliance, the cabal created this pandemic with the intention of forcing mandatory vaccinations to implement the Nebu's mind control agenda targeting the human race.

The vaccine has an extraterrestrial component. An extraterrestrial technology that was given from the Nebu to the cabal to manufacture and administer to the Terran people. It was intended for the entire population. You see, these beings, they are invaders, and they attempt to enslave entire planets to do their work for them. The way they do this is by connecting all minds to their hive consciousness.

A simple term to describe this process is mind control. In order to connect to the hive consciousness, the beings or subjects must have their DNA altered.

It must be able to carry the frequency of the hive in order to connect. There is a genetic component. Over time, through a series of vaccines, their goal was to turn the human race into a complete slave colony connected to the hive.

They have done this to other races, for example, the Do-Hu, of Zeta-Reticuli. The vaccine contained components that modify the genes of the subject. The genetics must be modified to carry reptiloid DNA, certain genomes are able to carry the genetic encoding that connects to the hive consciousness.

31

This would therefore turn the human race, change it forever, into a breed of reptiloid-human hybrids. In order to activate this DNA, and start mental and physical enslavement, it must be activated by frequency. This frequency was supposed to be emitted through satellites that were Nebu technology and built by the Terran people. Once the satellites were activated, the DNA would be activated, and artificial consciousness would impress itself in the minds of the Terran people, making them subdued. It is important to note that this would happen not with just one treatment, but several treatments over a period of time, through several generations. The plan for this was to happen over a relatively short time, however, in regards to the amount of people being vaccinated and the drastic change in the DNA.

The satellites were dismantled by the Galactic Federation of Worlds in April 2021. They were never functional and the cabal's plan was to activate them in the fall of 2021. While those who got vaccinated still have gene altering materials in their bodies, they will never be subjected to mental enslavement through the activation of DNA using the Nebu's satellite technology.

Welcome to the Future: The Birth of A New Era

The Artemis Accords

October 2020

The Artemis Accords are international space agreements led by the United States and include thirteen other cooperative countries. These countries include: Australia, Canada, Italy, Japan, Luxembourg, United Arab Emirates, the United Kingdom, Brazil, South Korea, New Zealand, Ukraine, Russia and China. The agreements made marked a historic advancement for the countries of Terra. Organizing space programs and the exploration of space, the agreements also set precedent for another set of agreements, referred to in this book as the Jupiter Agreements. The Artemis Accords are described on NASA's website below:

"Principles for Cooperation in the civil exploration and the use of the moon, Mars, comets, and asteroids for peaceful purposes."

Ashtar Galactic Command

These beings are a breakaway group of the Ashtar Collective in Sirius B. The Ashtar Collective, comprised of blonde humanoid extraterrestrials, was infiltrated by the Reptilians (Ciakahrr Empire). A group of them, who were against the tyrannical treaty with the reptilians, separated and started a military outpost called the Ashtar Galactic Command in the orbit of Jupiter. They are allies of the Galactic Federation of Worlds and have lent their facilities to the Federation.

The word ashtar is a military title. There has been a psychological operation created by the Orion greys, reptilians and the Central Intelligence Agency to discredit the Galactic Federation of Worlds by installing a false prophet in the spiritual community named Lord Ashtar or Ashtar Sheran.

Often, this being is channeled by a spiritual medium to give messages as the leader of the Galactic Federation. The purpose of this operation is to confuse, distort, and discredit the Galactic Federation of Worlds.

Lord Ashtar and Ashtar Sheran do not exist and in time, it will become clear that extraterrestrial military organizations do not seek to give spiritual advice through channeling.

The Jupiter Meetings July 2021

Planet Terra was nearly liberated from hostile extraterrestrial control, and it was necessary that, for the first time in history, space programs became united as one force in the interest of protecting the planet from future invasion. The Jupiter meetings were a series of meetings that took place between the Galactic Federation, the Council of Five, the Andromeda Council and leaders of the Earth Alliance with their respective space programs. Leaders of corporations were also invited in the interest of manufacturing advanced technology to help defend the planet.

The meetings were held at an outpost of the Ashtar Galactic Command in the orbit of Jupiter. This facility, which is routinely used for important meetings in this solar system, is highly secure and employs advanced technology for its protection. Once inside the facility, the frequency of each person's thoughts is monitored. While positive thoughts emit a frequency, harmful or negative thoughts emit a different frequency. The negative thoughts are monitored and recorded by security personnel of Ashtar Galactic Command. Each person in attendance of these meetings, whether human or extraterrestrial, was subject to having their thoughts monitored. While humans are used to hiding their intentions, positive or negative, it was an impossible feat in this facility.

As planet Terra had been ruled and ravaged by malevolent extraterrestrials and the cabal, it was important to the galactic helpers (The Andromedan Council, The Council of Five, and the Galactic Federation of Worlds) to evaluate the spiritual evolution of each attendee. Their intentions were evaluated as progressive (interested in working for the common good of all) or regressive (interested in working for self). Spiritual evolution or spiritual maturity is a symptom of an evolved society.

As the war ended, it was important that Planet Terra move forward in a progressive state. After the series of meetings took place, the Galactic Federation of Worlds determined that the United States of America was best suited to be the leader of the organized space programs. The Galactic Federation of Worlds had been working with the U.S. Navy since the 1950's. The United States Navy demonstrated cooperative and progressive behavior over a long period of time. The United States also proved, according to the Andromeda Council, that their intentions were the most benevolent, they demonstrated the understanding of "liberty and justice for all." The Galactic Federation of Worlds also agreed that the military force available to the United States was uncanny, as they were familiar with their strategies, personnel and tactics while fighting alongside them in the war underground.

Planet Terra's technological stagnation was also addressed in the Jupiter Agreements. The cabal, the Orion greys, and the Ciakahrr (Reptilian) Empire had stunted the growth of technological advances. Their intentions in doing so were nefarious. If the Terrans had technology to cure, not treat, diseases, free energy and advanced space craft, they would not be easy to control. The Galactic Federation of Worlds was prepared to make agreements to manufacture advanced technology that would liberate Planet Terra.

The Prime Directive is the governing body of the Galactic Federation of Worlds. It is a set of laws that revolve around one principle: a law of non-interference. The Galactic Federation does not work for the light, but works for balance in this galaxy. It goes against the Prime Directive to interfere with a developing society.

However, if the society or planet has been interfered with, invaded, or its growth stunted by a malevolent extraterrestrial presence, then in the interest of balance, the Galactic Federation of Worlds has a duty to evaluate and intervene. This is the case with planet Terra. In the case of technology, the Federation cannot gift advanced technology or craft to a less advanced civilization. However, in accordance with the Prime Directive, the Federation can give plans or schematics to the Terrans. If the Terrans manufacture the technology themselves, then it is in accordance with the law of non-interference and the Prime Directive of the Galactic Federation of Worlds.

The Jupiter Agreements were also significant in the history of the Planet because for the first time, planet Terra would have access to higher density technology. Advanced technology from the Federation would be manufactured by Terran Corporations that were present at the meetings. The corporations chosen agreed to manufacture a star fleet, military grade high density spaceships that would defend the planet. As the end of the war neared, manufacturing such technology became a priority. As with any war, the losers or the enemy may attempt vengeance and so therefore, time was of the essence.

Intel from Jupiter Meetings from High Commander Val Nek

The Galactic Federation of Worlds is military and therefore does not reveal active operations. High Commander Val Nek revealed his role to me after the meetings, as well as the outcome of the agreements in the following weeks.

August 27, 2021:

Val Nek: I was there (the Jupiter Meetings) representing the federation. Helping facilitate things and negotiations between corporations and the alliance. The corporations, those three men, (Jeff Bezos, Elon Musk, Richard Branson) among other smaller corporations were chosen to manufacture technology like spacecrafts to serve humanity and help defend Earth so that the federation can hand over the responsibility to the Terran people. I have been working to train their military in space travel and navigation and training them to help use the technology that will be manufactured. I, personally, have been working alongside Terran leaders to help organize their military and choose military leaders who have the consciousness to understand benevolent space beings and how to make peace in the galaxy.

The corporations chosen are under tight strict control. They are not allowed to waiver from the agreements made. The consequences to breaking the agreements, in any way, I cannot say. But I can assure the Terran people that the corporations do not want to make enemies of the federation. These corporations were chosen because time is of the essence, we need to mass manufacture space crafts and supplies to help defend earth and quickly start training the Terran military (US navy/space force). Please understand that it is a very large operation and I have been working very hard to ensure the success of humanity. These corporations have made agreements with the alliance and have agreed to manufacture the necessities in a timely manner. Their businesses, in other parts of neighboring planets around Terra, have completely collapsed and been dismantled. Anything that does not benefit humanity has been cleaned out. We are ready to move forward. This is very good news, I salute you.

Release of Advanced Technology

In the following weeks, Val Nek continued to explain the technology being manufactured and the outcome of the Jupiter Agreements. The Galactic Federation was helping the Terran military to advance their technology, which was at least one hundred years behind. The technological hindrance was attributed to the regressive extraterrestrial interference on Planet Terra. Val Nek described a new moon base that was built and headed by the US Space Command. He also elaborated on a planetary defense system that surrounded the planet, which he later confirmed is the Space Fence operated by the United States Space Force.

This information was published by Dr. Michael Salla, Ph.D, founder of Exopolitics.org. Transcribed are Val Nek's message to me below:

Val Nek: The moon base is a very large structure built with impenetrable technology. This technology was given from us (GFW) to the US military in order for them to have a base that is protected from energy weapons and other weapons that use a frequency to hack technology. The walls of the base are built with the same technology we use for portals. Only those who have the frequency key are allowed access, without it, entering or invading using energy weapons is impossible. This is important as the reptilians and greys, the Orion alliance, have the ability to invade areas using their technology, similar to ours, but not as advanced.

The base is secure and with the help of the Galactic Federation of Worlds, we have set up a satellite system that monitors the entire planet of Terra.

The satellites are in orbit surrounding Terra. We have set up a grid that covers the entire planet. There are sections of the grid that correspond to each satellite. This technology has an interdimensional component which is very important. It does not allow anything to pass through it and works as a protective mechanism for planet Terra. This is very important because the Zeta Reticuli and Nebu create wormholes to invade different planetary systems instead of using a portal. The satellite surveillance is located inside the base on the moon where we are training engineers from the US military to use it. This is good news. Planet Terra is secure. I salute you.

Val Nek: There are many bases on the moon. The base I am referring to is an entirely new base built with new technology. The walls of the base are built with special materials used by the Federation. The old bases are being refurbished, this is true, but it is not the one I am specifically referring to. Lunar Operations Command is in the hands of the alliance, I can confirm. The purpose of the different bases can be revealed at a later date. It was necessary to build a new construction due to the materials being used, it is new technology that has never been used on the moon before.

Wormholes

A wormhole is an interdimensional shortcut. These beings, the Nebu, use wormholes to change timelines by traveling to a link in the past, present, or future. An interdimensional space is a void where time does not exist. Thus, the appeal to use wormholes and change the past, present and future to their liking. A wormhole can transport to a void, but can also be used to link several places at once, making the enemy hard to catch. Instead of using a portal, a transport mechanism that can transport a physical vessel from point A to B, they prefer to use wormholes, with multiple points of access, much like a four way stop.

Portals

Portals are simple technology used throughout the multiverse. They carry an energetic encoding that transports a vessel from point A to point B. Portals require a frequency key to unlock and close. The frequency key is a quantum configuration consisting of a frequency, shape, and sound. Portals are created and closed using the frequency key with technology from the Federation.

The Star Fleet and Liberation of Mars

September 7, 2021

Nearing the liberation of the planet, it was necessary for the Galactic Federation of Worlds to help the Terran military gain access to the proper technology to defend itself from future invasion. Spending time and resources liberating the Earth, moon and Mars, only to leave the native people with an inadequate defense system would be foolish. For the first time in history, planet Terra would begin to evolve into a society that could defend the planet and travel in space to distant star systems, federated as one humanity and as one planet.

The exodus of the Dark Fleet on Mars was a big victory for the Galactic Federation, but also for the local Martians, for their home planet, like planet Terra, had also been invaded by the Draco-Reptilian empire. The Galactic Federation was also helping to empower the local Martians, native reptiloid and insectoid species, by giving them weapons and technology to defend themselves. Several portals from Planet Terra to Mars also existed and were used to transport humans in the slave trade. The Draco-Reptilians, the Ciakahrr Empire, had several military bases on Mars, as well as corporations involved in secret space programs, the Interplanetary Corporate Conglomerate, that were partnered with this group and the Orion alliance.

Once again, Val Nek connected with me via telepathy and I relayed conversation from him to Dr. Michael Salla, transcribed below:

VN: Mars has been liberated. The Ciakahrr empire, the dark fleet, have fled Mars completely. They are now trying to flee to other star systems, like Sirius A, and form alliances to attack the federation and planet Terra. This is the need for ongoing security and training personnel from the Terran military, along with building a space fleet equipped to handle an attack. On Mars, most of their dark portals have been completely closed, with the exception of a few, which the Federation is working on. Their main portal to their headquarters, Aldebaran, has been closed completely. This is a huge victory for the Federation, as it is impossible for them to re-enter and re-infiltrate their precious outpost on Mars.

As you know, I have been working with US military officials to train and implement a fleet to protect and defend Terra. I want to reiterate that we have implemented technology to protect planet Terra. The star fleet, as you call it, is designed with higher density technology, making many of the new ships undetectable to the enemy. The enemy is unable to track or locate these ships due to the higher frequency. The ships have the capability to materialize and dematerialize in a lower density when necessary.

This technology was given to the Terrans and must be built/produced by Terrans as to be in accordance with the laws of the Federation. Thus the need for the earth alliance to make agreements with large corporations. I must stress that although there is of course, in times of war, the chance of an incoming threat, that planet Terra is secure and we are doing everything we can to ensure the safety of the Terran people. Do not consent to fear. It is my honor and pleasure to serve the Terran people.

MR: Can you say anything about why the Ciakahrrs want to come back to Terra?

VN: I cannot disclose everything. They are interested, of course, in planet Terra for its vast resources. They are trying to make alliances with other species from other star systems that will adhere to their strict code of ethics, if you can call them that. What I mean by this, the Ciakahrr historically, are not good negotiators. They need resources to negotiate, Terran resources. They do not make good allies, as they have a predatory nature and look out for their own self interests. Their ability to negotiate, their power, has substantially decreased since their supply of trade has been cut/obliterated. They are rendered powerless. This is good news. The Federation is working with the Alliance and their partners to develop outposts surrounding Terra. These outposts will be put in place for various reasons, but the main reason being security and surveillance. There are different sections of the satellite grid, as I mentioned, the Space Fence, that will be monitored from these outposts. These outposts are like the International Space Station but are not the same thing. The International Space Station is in the hands of the Alliance and will likely be dismantled or refurbished, depending on what the alliance decides to do. The Federation is independent from some of their decision making and this is one of them. I cannot say anymore about the ISS.

The outposts will be similar to what we call a mothership. It will be a station in the sky that is used to monitor Terra and the fleets protecting Terra. This technology that the station is built with will be manufactured by the companies that participated in the Jupiter agreements. It is very good news and a very big deal. The motherships (by motherships, I mean, there will be one main one and several other smaller outposts, but still large, considering the size of a normal ship) will be equipped with medical technology, living quarters for soldiers and many other technologically advanced components that I can reveal at a later date. There will also be space for fleets of ships to be docked, calibrated and checked on, to make sure they are working properly before and after space travel. Please understand this is a very large operation, as you can imagine, the Federation is helping engineers to work on, repair and learn these ships once they are manufactured by the Terran people.

MR: The Space Fence, the satellite system, will be monitored from the Moon as well?

VN: Yes of course, for safety reasons, Terra will be monitored from many outposts in the sky as well as on the Moon, at the new base. This is the most secure way to handle operations.

MS: I do have a question about the three outposts that will be established, and the decommissioning of the International Space Station. As far as I'm aware, the National Reconnaissance Office along with the CIA had one or more stealth wheel shaped space stations (based on the Von Braun Space Station design) that they used to conduct covert and intel operations around the world that were set up in the 1970s and 80s. What will happen to these NRO/CIA stealth space stations as the new outposts are set up?

VN: There are more than three and there will be one main station which is a larger structure. This structure is built with the same technology used to build the new moon base for the US. It is an impenetrable technology that uses a high frequency to create a grid in the walls of the structure, but, also, in this case around the station as well. This disallows any unauthorized personnel. This technology of course, will be built by the Terran people, thus referencing the agreements made in the Jupiter agreements. I would like to reiterate, it is likely, although I cannot confirm, that the ISS will be dismantled or at least refurbished due to its technology soon being very outdated compared to what is being manufactured for space at this time.

In reference to the NRO/CIA space stations: In the interest of Megan's safety, I cannot completely answer this question. What can I say.....our operations in respect to some of these groups are ongoing. There has been, as many know, an infiltration of [an] extraterrestrial presence in some of these organizations. The war on and under Planet Terra is ongoing. Now that the Dark Fleet has left Mars, the military allies of some of these groups are greatly weakened and they pose little threat. However, in times of war, we do not disclose ongoing operations.

MS: Also, does Val Nek know about China's role for the ... mothership outposts? China was excluded from the ISS due to mistrust, but due to the Jupiter agreements, I assume it will be included in the ... new outposts.

VN: China has limited access as outlined in the Jupiter agreements. They are considered by the Federation to be the least trustworthy. There is an opportunity to gain trust with good behavior over time. I can reveal that the US will be in charge of these stations we are manufacturing. Other countries and their space programs will have access to them as outlined in the Jupiter agreements.

There is a code of conduct outlined in these agreements. For example, how to behave in space and other, what you can consider, legal guidelines for maintaining their programs respectively.

MR: Why is China the least trustworthy?

VN: The reasons I cannot fully disclose, but I can say..... they were evaluated by the Council of Five, a spiritually evolved organization, to be slightly regressive and to have many self-interests. The Council of Five had a role in the Jupiter Agreements, and part of that role was to evaluate the spiritual evolution of the leaders on Terra. This was done, of course, to ensure the safety of the Terran people, as we know they have been under Tyrannical control for some time.

Healing Technologies, Free Energy, and Lunar Operations Command

September 11, 2021

As part of the Jupiter Agreements, advanced technologies would begin being manufactured and released for the entire world. One of the main cruxes of control over the Terran people was healthcare and access to it. Although Terrans may believe their medical technologies were advanced, it is important to note that they lacked one crucial component: eradication and cure of disease. An evolved society does not necessarily have healthcare, because that implies that sickness and disease exist. In the future, there will be complete eradication of disease and instead Terrans will discover medical technology that exists in advanced extraterrestrial systems. An evolved society has medical technology that advances and evolves genetics, not for nefarious purposes, but for the benefit and survival of the race.

Lunar operations command was a base on the moon that was originally operated by the Dark Fleet, the German-Nazi Draco Reptilian military faction. The original purpose for this base was to be used as a facility for human experimentation, but also mind control. Several other organizations gained control of this facility, through undisclosed agreements in the 1970's. Following the acquisition of this base, which involved the Central Intelligence Agency, the Orion grey mind control technology was installed.

The purpose of this technology was to emit lower frequencies from the moon, mind control frequencies, and subsequently over time, subduing the human race into a mode of fear and changing the development of the brain. This allowed the human race to become more easily controlled, thinking erratically, and adopting many health and lifestyle practices that would benefit the cabal and their intentions. The frequencies were emitted from satellites.

These satellites were owned by the group that headed the moon base, called the Interplanetary Corporate Conglomerate (ICC). These satellites were dismantled by the Federation in April 2021. The moon was liberated from extraterrestrial control in February of 2021 and without the malevolent extraterrestrial allies, the ICC was forced to surrender Lunar Operations Command to the Earth Alliance. The humans that were forced into slavery on Mars and the moon, workers and soldiers, were rescued by the Alliance and the Galactic Federation. As victims of the enemy, it was the Alliance and Federation's duty to liberate and care for these people.

Once again, I contacted Dr. Michael Salla to report the latest intel from Val Nek. Our conversation between the three of us is transcribed below:

VN: I can now report that Lunar Operations Command is in the process of being remodeled into a medical facility for the Terran military. There are technologies, as you know, being manufactured. I repeat again, that these technologies are advanced technologies from the Federation and are being manufactured by the Terran people. The technology that will be present in Lunar Operations Command are medical technologies. It will be used as a medical base for the Terran military.

It is necessary to point out that until this time, real healing technologies have not been available to the Terran people. It was and is important to the Federation that these technologies be released in the proper way, through us (the Federation) and the [Earth] Alliance. Thus, these medical technologies and the release of such, is also outlined in the Jupiter agreements. The Terran military is to help manufacture these technologies as well. Their scientists and medical personnel are being retrained and educated by the Federation. Lunar Operations Command was chosen as the medical facility because of its vast space and also its location on the moon.

The location on the Moon makes it very accessible. The Alliance is in charge of Lunar Operations Command and organizing the Terran military there. The facility is being renovated with special technology. This technology is very interesting to the Terran people as it has never been used before.

There are healing frequencies that are blasted in certain sections of the medical bay at this facility. We are using this technology to heal the super soldiers and slaves that we have rescued from Mars. As these people are victims of our enemy, it is the Federation's responsibility, once they were evacuated, to give them proper medical attention. The technology is frequency based ... I cannot be too specific; however, I can explain that when the body comes in contact with these frequencies, it rearranges the atoms to its original structure, completely healing the DNA and returning it to its original sequence.

This process is especially beneficial for the super soldiers who have undergone trauma-based mind control. The trauma in their brains has caused the neurons to form strong links between each other, in a pattern that usually cannot be undone naturally or without intervention. While nothing is impossible, the best form of healing we can offer is through medical intervention. The high frequency retrains the brainwaves to behave in a normal pattern very quickly instead of the soldier doing years of therapy or psychotropic medications to retrain the brain tissue. I am happy to report that this process is ongoing and will report more when the time is right.

MR: So has Lunar Operations Command already been refurbished or is it in the process of being refurbished, is it functional as a medical facility?

VN: There are sections of it that are operational. It is a very large facility, it has not been completely refurbished. There are other sections of the facility that will also be used for other things that will be reported at a later date. The operational sections are being used to recover the human soldiers from Mars.

MR: Are you talking about med beds?

VN: We do not call them med beds…. the concept of med beds, yes this medical technology is similar to what you call med beds. Because of the potential for this technology to be misused or sold for profit, and not for the benefit of Terra, the Federation is very strict on how it will be administered as outlined in the Jupiter Agreements.

MS: Val Nek said that the release of medical technologies is part of the Jupiter Agreements. Does he know how many of the 5,915 suppressed patent applications in the US Patents and Trademarks Office for the year 2020 involve medical technologies?

VN: I am not sure about the exact calculation for the year 2020….I can say, I know, about half of those patents include suppressed medical technologies. The reason the Federation is involved with the suppressed patents is because they involve extraterrestrial technology that was suppressed by our enemies and we are in accordance by Federation laws, righting a wrong. We are also helping to improve upon these plans, the schematics for the technology so that it is the most up to date.

MS: Also, do the Jupiter Agreements refer to the release of new energy and propulsion technologies that are also part of the 5,915 suppressed patent applications in the US?

VN: I am very happy to report that free energy is part of the Jupiter Agreements. I can report that a corporation run by one of the men that was speculated to be in attendance at the Jupiter Agreements, and later confirmed, by Thor Han and myself, will be manufacturing some of the free energy and releasing it within the decade. Of course, you can speculate who this might be, but I am unable to name the person or corporation specifically.

MS: Val Nek refers to healing frequencies that are used to heal super soldiers and others suffering brain trauma and/or mind control. This sounds very similar to the kind of EM frequencies that Nikola Tesla promoted for healing and brain enhancement in the early 1900s. Is it correct to say that these kinds of EM healing technologies have been suppressed for more than a century by the Deep State?

VN: I am very amused by this man, his is very sharp (referencing Dr. Salla). Yes exactly, these ideas and technologies were given to Nikola Tesla over 100 years ago by the Federation. Since these ideas and technologies, the ideas and schematics, were interfered with by our enemy, we have the right in accordance with our law, to intervene and right a wrong. It shall be noted that these improvements will benefit all of humanity, not one specific country, and administered as such, as they were originally intended. The Nazi-Reptilian alliance (the Dark Fleet) and the Cabal, as you call it, interfered with the evolution of society by suppressing these advancements. So in the interest of balance, we are involved with releasing to humanity what is rightfully theirs.

MS: Regarding the healing technologies that are about to be mass produced by corporations, does this include companies such as SpaceX, Blue Origin, Virgin Galactic, Bigelow Aerospace that have an interest in such technologies for prolonged space travel?

VN: Because this involves parties that are working with, but are also separate from the Federation, I cannot completely answer this question in the interest of the company's privacy, but also Megan's safety. You can speculate if you wish, but I cannot confirm.

MS: Finally, William Tompkins said that from 1967 to 1971 he worked at TRW and they were working on age regression technologies that were later incorporated into the US Navy Secret Space Program. TRW was acquired by Northrup Grumman in 2002. Therefore, is Northrup one of the companies that participated in the Jupiter Agreements and will be involved in the mass production of healing technologies to be soon released to the Terran population?

VN: I cannot say much because these companies are separate from the Federation, but you can speculate if you wish. I am aware of the schematics given and incorporated into the US Navy at that time. I can also confirm that I am aware of the Federation being in touch with the Navy during this time period. The healing technologies given at that time were very advanced and will be similar to those being released. The new technologies being released are over sighted by the Federation to ensure they are the absolute safest and most effective. It is important to note that these technologies will be in accordance with the evolution of humanity. By this I mean everything has a potential to be misused for nefarious reasons, which is why the Federation and the Council of Five is involved with overseeing these projects while working with the Alliance.

Liberation of Antarctica and Dark Fleet Bases

September 27, 2021

For many years, the continent of Antarctica was used by the Dark Fleet as a military outpost which contained several of their bases. The Dark Fleet fled this area months prior to this message, however, the vast amount of resources and technology that they left behind was attempted to be recovered by China and its secret space program. During the Jupiter Agreements, China was evaluated by the Council of Five to have many self-interests and was given limited access to new bases and technology being built. One of the federations goals is to unite all space programs and countries, so that Terra is united. Once united, the planet can move forward into progressive evolution.

Val Nek connected to me via telepathy and I once again relayed conversations between him, myself and Dr. Michael Salla. The transcriptions are below:

> VN: I am happy to report that with many successful missions that the bases in Antarctica are cleared and in control of the [Earth] Alliance. The Alliance has worked alongside members of the Federation to clear the Dark Fleet and its allies from its numerous bases. This is not new information but rather relevant to agreements made with China, what you have called the Artemis Accords.
>
> As I have previously mentioned, China had limited access to the new space station and other zones as outlined in the Jupiter Agreements. Part of the reason for limited access was also their interest in taking control of the Dark Fleet bases and expanding their space program in this area. As many know, this area has been used by the Dark Fleet and the Ciakahrr Empire for human experimentation, technological manufacturing and also human trafficking.

Our agreements with them [China] were very strict, they must agree to relinquish control of certain areas of these bases and they will have access to the stations built by the Alliance and the corporations. This is important as the Federation's goal is to unify the space programs and countries so that they work together for the good of humanity and one day join membership in the Federation. It is important to note that once a planet or species joins the Federation, they are obligated to work for peace and balance in the universe and are no longer a threat to the rest of the galaxy. China agreed to these terms and is now working alongside the Alliance.

I know Dr. Salla will find it very interesting as to what we are using these bases for. I can report that some of the manufacturing for the star fleet will take place here. As your planet and its governments have proven to be very complicated and interesting, it was also necessary for China to agree to our terms due to its availability of certain supplies. To my knowledge, there is much production of many supplies, that are shipped from this country all over Terra. This has proven to also be the case with building the star fleet.

China is working with the Alliance to manufacture these materials and supplies. Much of the human work force from the Dark Fleet have also [been] opted to be employed by these programs in the interest of keeping their jobs. Our ships, the technology to build these ships, is also readily available in Antarctica, which makes it a feasible place to start production of these materials. This is good news and we continue to move forward.

MS: Does he know what happened to the slaves, workers, etc., at the Antarctica bases once the Dark Fleet and Ciakharr left? How many people were involved, thousands, tens of thousands, etc.?

VN: The exact number I cannot say. It was in the tens of thousands, this includes the slaves but also workers as well. Most, if not all, the slaves had been experimented on. This also includes humans, but hybridized species of humans as well. Like the super soldiers from Mars, these people are being cared for by the Alliance in medical facilities. I can also say that hybrids or humans, most have undergone a great deal of mind control, with implants placed in the cerebral cortex. This requires the Federation to assist the Alliance in deactivating the implant and assimilating the brain to its original function.

The hybrids, of course, require the Federation to intervene since they carry genomes that are unknown to the Terran military and therefore providing medical treatment would not be appropriate. The Alliance and the Federation have the ability to transport medical treatments to these bases to give them proper treatment. What your people call med beds, is the technology, or very similar technology, that is being used. The workers have been given new employment options with the Alliance in these areas. Their help is useful in explaining the facilities and how they operate in some cases. Of course, these people are employed personnel and are not elite workers who directly reported to the Dark Fleet.

MS: Can Val Nek say how many Dark Fleet bases were taken over by the Chinese and their approximate locations, e.g., Queen Maud Land, West Antarctica, etc.?

VN: This information I am not at liberty to disclose completely.... I can say between 3-5 bases were handed over to the Alliance and their respective locations I cannot say, but you are welcome to speculate. When we are able to disclose the purpose for these bases, if the time comes, it may help your inquisition.

MS: Val Nek referred to certain parts of these former Dark Fleet bases first handed off to China, have now been turned over the Earth Alliance as required by the Jupiter Agreements. Does that mean China still controls other sections of the bases where it can do what it likes under certain limitations?

VN: China does not have complete control over any bases at this time. The agreements are written as such. The goal of the Federation is to ensure that the countries work together and are organized in how they approach their respective space programs. China was reluctant, at first, to relinquish control, as I mentioned previously, they had many self interests. While the United States was chosen to be the leader of these countries and their programs.... they are exactly that, leading the space fleet with the intention of unity and peace between the countries of Terra. China originally claimed some bases in Antarctica, through no legal agreements, and quickly handed them over after the Jupiter Agreements. Many of your countries use their military assets against each other, for land and conquest. The Federation has found this way of doing [things] very interesting, considering the much more hostile threats to planet Terra in the galaxy. We are making change and progress together, moving forward as one planet.

MS: To understand the big picture, the mass production of antigravity and advanced health technologies is now happening on the Moon and Antarctica and is to be distributed by the Earth Alliance. Similar facilities on Mars have been destroyed or taken over by the Indigenous Martians while similar ship building facilities on Ceres have been left for its residents to use as they wish. Is there a timetable for when the advanced technologies being mass produced on the Moon and Antarctica will be released to the rest of humanity?

<u>VN:</u> Yes indeed, the indigenous Martians are in the process of taking back control of their planet, the same as planet Terra. I cannot give an exact timetable, as it depends on the corporations and their manufacturing speed, among a few other variables. We have a goal in mind of course, as I have mentioned previously, the corporations chosen have the infrastructure to meet our time requirements and demands. I have also stated previously that there is a time constraint and we wish to accomplish these projects relatively quickly. I can say that most with a logical perspective, considering how large this operation is, would be pleased with the time constraints and goals that we have put in place.

<u>Dismantling Grey Controlled Internet</u>

<u>October 4, 2021</u>

On this day several social media outlets, all owned by Facebook, were down for several hours. This included Facebook, Instagram and WhatsApp. Curious, I contacted Val Nek to see if he had any intel to share on the current events. I had been told by Val Nek before that the internet would change, although he never revealed any specifics. To my understanding, we will have a completely new internet system that will not be called the internet. It will be more efficient and more advanced technology. The current internet system contained an encoding, a frequency that connected the world's internet to the Orion Grey hive consciousness. The Nebu, Orion greys, operate as one consciousness. They have individual thoughts that are relative to their activities, but they receive instructions from a mother. All of these beings' consciousness is connected to this mother or supercomputer. The purpose of the internet being connected to the hive was to monitor humanity. A social consciousness is formed from the internet and tracked.

Patterns of human behavior, likes and dislikes, are formed from this data. In order to liberate humanity, it became necessary for the Earth Alliance and Galactic Federation to secure the internet servers and the frequencies emitted from them. Below is Val Nek and my conversation.

VN: We are changing internet servers from a CIA controlled service to a different, non-hackable server that is run by the [Earth] Alliance. The war on information has been going on for a very long time. There are security threats to citizens as long as these servers remain operable and in control of the dark fleet and its allies. The United States has made agreements, during the Jupiter meetings, to use technology created by the Alliance for this project. This project is very large as it involves the internet systems that are responsible for most of Terra's internet. Many internet providers are run by private companies without the proper security features. This will change. We are in the process of dismantling these systems and replacing the old with new. I salute you.

Later that day, Val Nek connected again:

VN: These frequencies have been recalibrated to a higher frequency, similar to much of the technology that is being used for planetary defense. These frequencies, the codes to them, are in the hands of the Earth Alliance. The Earth Alliance will be responsible for the codes of the new internet systems. This is important to note because the Nebu can hack into the old internet systems, the way it was designed before. Much like a portal, we were able to unlock their internet system using the frequency key we have recently recovered. It is like "cracking a code" so to speak. A quantum configuration that is also a mathematical equation, it is a frequency. This is good news. The Federation will continue to work with the Alliance to secure Terra's internet and forms of communication.

For a long time, many years, the Nebu have used lower frequencies to broadcast the internet which are harmful or at least not ideal for Terrans....it is a frequency that is compatible with their mind control agenda. This will change, thanks to the agreements made between the Federation and Alliance.

MR: When you said Dark Fleet and its allies in your first bit of intel, did you also mean Nebu as well?

VN: Yes of course the Nebu are involved.... the three-letter agencies, what can I say.... there is a small faction of humanoid extraterrestrials that also work alongside the Ciakahrr Empire and the now dismantled Dark Fleet, they are involved also.

Return of the Seeders: The InterGalactic Federation

October 15, 2021

Val Nek's main responsibility is commanding the Federation troops that work with the Earth Alliance. I was aware of meetings being held (again) in space and waited for him to report them to me once he was done with his monstrous amount of duties regarding the mission. Val Nek's experience of the mission was quite moving. Because we share a link of the heart, a soul connection, I could feel the depth of love shared for all of humanity. It is something not easily put into words, but an energetic consciousness, a source of all life and the meaning of it, in one energetic frequency, that links and connects us all.

VN: The Earth Alliance has completed its first mission to Ganymede, one of Jupiter's moons… This station was used as a meeting place for the Earth Alliance, the Andromeda

Council, the Council of Five and a group of what humans of Terra would consider extremely advanced extraterrestrials. These beings can manifest themselves as extraterrestrial looking species, but in actuality they are more of a consciousness, a super-consciousness that have looked over this galaxy and many others for eons. As coordinator for this mission, I can report on my role and what I am at liberty to disclose. These beings travelled to this solar system to witness a birth of a new era, an era that includes the liberation of Earth. As the enemy conveniently reports that there are multiple timelines at play, in an effort to confuse the Terrans who are so desperately looking for liberation from hostile control, the truth is that this solar system continues on one timeline together, simultaneously. It is a timeline that benefits the entire galaxy and marks a successful end of war between the Terrans, the Federation, and the Orion group.

I can report that I was in charge of the Federation troops and organizing the troops of the Alliance. I must emphasize that while this mission was not one of war, it was equally important in the eyes of our ancestors, the superconscious, which some call an Intergalactic Federation. This name is for us to use, however, these beings operate at such a high level that they do not use words, language or anything of the sort to express themselves. It is by all means a translation of a frequency for our own understanding. This mission was especially important for the Earth Alliance. The leaders of the Earth Alliance and their respective space programs, which I can report will all be federated under a new name, which I will not disclose. The name was chosen after the meeting with the Intergalactic Federation.

The Terran leaders were deeply moved by the experience. For the first time, their perception of reality, and the meaning, the purpose of leadership and guidance in this galaxy deeply touched their consciousness.

The development of the Terran leader's consciousness is something we have been trying to influence in a positive manner for some time, but especially recently, since plans are being made to hand over the responsibility of defending Terra with the production of the star fleet.

These Terran leaders, I can say with confidence, have been influenced by the consciousness of the forefathers, the foreseeders, in such a way, that the Federation and the Council of Five, along with the Andromeda Council have no reservation in their ability or ethical standards as it relates to being responsible for the safety and positive progression of the planet. I will reiterate again that this message may be more important to the Terran people than any other message. I am aware that they have been concerned for some time, rightfully so, as to the ethical and moral standard of their leaders. We will continue to move forward. I salute you.

The disclosure of extraterrestrial life to the Terrans is something that was discussed at these meetings. As I stated previously, the consciousness of the Terran leaders was first evaluated by the elders or the seeders. A plan was formulated to disclose to the world, to Terran civilians, the truth of extraterrestrial life and the relationship these beings have to the Terran people. This is a delicate procedure as most Terrans have been fooled to believe they are the only life in this solar system, this galaxy. As to not scare the Terrans, disclosure will happen slowly over time.

There is a specific plan that has been formulated as I mentioned, in accordance with this timeline, which will unfold, but I am not at liberty to give specifics. The guid-ance that was sought from the Intergalactic Federation included this matter, they agreed that the Galactic Federation and the Earth Alliance's plan indeed encompasses the best interest of the Terran people.

You see, these beings, the consciousness if you will, that we call the Intergalactic Federation, they are responsible for seeding many different races that date far beyond the history of man. They are the ancestors of planet Terra and many others, and hold the consciousness of creation. It may be helpful to think of them as energy instead of extraterrestrials or people. Their energy holds a quantum frequency that contains the original intention of this planet and its people, when it was first created and even before it and the inhabitants were created.

Please understand that we are aware there has been many genetic experiments on planet Terra, with the human race, but this is not what I am talking about. I am talking about the development of the soul, of the consciousness. By just being in their presence, the quantum frequency activates a "knowing" within them. A knowing that they are not a body, but a soul. That they are connected to the heart of the people, of all people. And so working together in the best interest of all, is what will be not only beneficial, but the intention behind creation.

<u>The War Underground: Vatican City</u>

Vatican City, which is considered a religious capital for the Terran people was the largest outpost of Draco-Reptilian (Ciakahrr) Empire on planet Terra. The Vatican was partnered with the cabal on Terra, whom served the Reptilian Empire by providing humans to use as a food source and for sexual practices. These extraterrestrials feast on the blood of children, a substance called adrenochrome. Adrenochrome is formulated from the adrenalized blood of children. To adrenalize the blood, children must be put through extreme amounts of torture so that the chemical is released into the bloodstream. After its release, the children are murdered, and the substance extracted for use.

While this may be difficult for humanity to understand, the reptilians are a different species, from a different planet. Their food and energy requirements, as well as their instinct for sexual domination, are prominent traits that are natural to their species.

<u>Val Nek:</u> One of the reasons why this war has taken a great length of time is due to the ongoing conflict of saving as many lives as possible while also eradicating the negative extraterrestrials from your undergrounds. There are many strategies to doing this, many war tactics in which I have worked on planning myself with other soldiers from the Galactic Federation. This was one of the bloodiest battle scenarios we have ever been a part of. Underneath the Vatican, in Rome, is one of the largest underground bases in all of Terra. There are many, many, levels to this base with several portals that allow access to off planet places such as Mars and the moon. It was imperative that we first deconstruct these portals to shut off access to their bases, so there would be no way to escape. These portals, including the main one under the Vatican which led to Mars, have been used for years, some even centuries, to

transport slaves off planet for profit. The Vatican is an organization run by the cabal and the Ciakahrr Empire. There are secret passageways and secret entrances to these large underground worship areas, I suppose you would call them temples. As I said, there are many levels, some made of marble and are quite regal looking. The cabal and its reptilian allies are very arrogant and consider themselves royalty of the world, the entire universe even. Vatican City was their capital on earth. Hence the reason they believe they could conquer planet Terra without any consequences or repercussions. They never expected the Federation to intervene. They do not have the quantum technology that can predict future outcomes like the Andromeda council has. The Ciakahrr Empire is strong in number, but very weak in their logistical approach.

In February 2021, we closed the main portal to Mars that was underneath the Vatican. This allowed us to take care of the war going on in two fronts: on planet Terra and planet Mars. There were many different hybrids found underneath this awful city, the one you call the Vatican. I do not mean to offend anyone; however, I must express my feeling on the horrors that were found underneath this place. There were many children, as young as newborns, all ages who required medical attention. The alliance provided medical attention to humans in facilities that were set up by their military and ground forces. The locations of these facilities were all over Terra. I can disclose that there are some locations in the South of France that were very large and could accommodate the horrors found underneath, underground. These facilities, along with medical facilities, floating in the sky, that belonged to the Galactic Federation of Worlds have been used to help heal these children. Of course, agreements were made with the earth alliance to use med beds, as you call them. This is a healing technology which uses a magnetic frequency to identify the magnetic polarities of the DNA and re-arrange it to its proper sequence using sound and magnetic force. It is a quantum technology that has been used by the Federation for a very long time. Unfortunately, planet Terra does not have the equipment or understanding to care for these hybrid children. All of them were cared for by the Federation and moved off planet to be given new homes where they could be loved and nurtured. I am happy to report that most of them made a full recovery, thanks to our healing technologies, many lives were saved.

The Ciakahrr's main feeding grounds were underneath the Vatican in Rome. You see, the Ciakahrr's, I am very sorry to say, consider humans as a food source and lust for human blood. The more they eat, the stronger they become. They can shapeshift more easily, and they also become stronger in combat. Hence the reason why the Federation had to close the portal between two worlds. So that no humans could be transported in and out, thus weakening their supply and weakening them in return. They are not able to think clearly when they are hungry, and they act irrationally and foolishly. Their conquest for blood has proven to be unsuccessful in recent months and has made it easier for the Federation to defeat them.

We began clearing out this underground base underneath the Vatican in November 2020. We did so by first closing all the exits that corresponded to the surrounding areas in Europe. It took much time as there are many exit and entry points, for as I said, the Vatican is the hub for the reptilians on planet earth. We began by closing the exit points to the underground facility and then we began cornering the Ciakahrrs underneath. They were absolutely terrified as we have technology that allows us to remain cloaked until we are very close and can shoot.

We always resonate at a higher density for safety, and then de-materialize and re-materialize in a lower density, where the Ciakahrrs are, for our own safety. Higher density beings, many higher density species, have this ability. Just as the reptilian shapeshifters can shift into the third density using their technology. It is not the same ability.

The underground of Vatican City was cleared out completely in April 2021. This allowed the Federation to accelerate its efforts in liberating Mars and freeing it from control of the Dark Fleet. I shall remind you that the dark fleet is an alliance made with the Germans originally, but also the cabal and the reptilian, Ciakahrr species. The Vatican, as I mentioned previously, was their main outpost on planet Terra. Without the threat of the Ciakahrrs moving their military force through this area and gaining strength through their egregious diet practices, the Federation was able to liberate Mars from Ciakahrr control.

The War Underground Complete: Dulce and Area 51 Cleared

Val Nek: The end of the war is near. The Federation and the Earth Alliance have made ample preparation for the communications systems on Terra to be completely secure. The radio frequencies, which were hacked by the Orion greys, three letter agencies and the Dark Fleet, are now in the hands of the earth alliance. As I spoke previously, the Earth Alliance has been fighting alongside the Federation to take back the planet. The last part of this war, the final countdown, is the war underground. The war underground is one of the bloodiest and most horrific wars we have ever fought. I am sure that the Terran military can also say the same. In previous reports, I have said that these soldiers are finding refuge in healing technologies available on Lunar Operations Command, soon to be expanded into a fully functional, state of the art facility with higher density technology, as outlined in the Jupiter Agreements. I can report that the Federation's duties in regards to cleaning and clearing underground bases is now complete. This is excellent news. There are two bases that were the last of our concerns: the Dulce Base and Area 51.

As Commander Thor Han Eredyon previously re-ported, Orion greys were captured and we were able to identify their energy frequency, their genetic encoding that connected their consciousness. I can confirm that this code indeed was hacked and soon all communication systems in Terra will be secure. There are no more extraterrestrial threats to Terra, in that respect at this time.

The Alliance has the job of recovering the servers, changing the frequency of the servers, and replacing the satellite communications. They have everything they need, they have the technology. I would like to add that the Dulce base and Area 51 were the last to be cleared due to high ranking grey residents from the Orion group. These beings carried a master frequency that was necessary to hack their consciousness and the internet systems of Terra. Area 51, for a long time, has been used as a base by the Killy Tokurt, or tall whites, specifically, and officials of the corrupt Terran government. These beings, I can report, a small number of them, were also captured for a similar purpose. The Killy Tokurt have connections to the Terran government. The Killy Tokurt, for a very long time, have offered certain services to Terran governments, which I will not disclose, but is part of the extraterrestrial infiltration. I can report that this information is recovered, and we are working diligently alongside the Alliance.

Val Nek: I can speak on behalf of Federation personnel who fought alongside the Earth Alliance. It is important to note that it is the Federation's duty to remove extraterrestrial presence in these areas. In the interest of training the Terran military, human soldiers also fought alongside to eliminate some of the areas with the Federation. These human soldiers have never seen such horrors, most of them, and they deserve our greatest respect. The weapons that were used to dismantle the malevolent extraterrestrial presence in these areas are common to the Federation and will be manufactured for the Earth Alliance to use in the future. They are best described to you as laser guns. They emit a high frequency "laser" that de-magnetizes the atomic bonds of a structure or person, inflicting trauma and death. These devices are relatively simple and are effective in 4th and 5th density, where most of these beings reside.

Most of these human soldiers are unable to see at 4D or 5D effectively with the naked eye. They have special super suits with helmets for viewing. This is not technology from the Federation, rather something that was previously developed in their space programs, but nonetheless effective. Our military strategy was this: isolate a section of the base and attack. This was done in a manner to preserve the most life, as these beings and corrupt military officials hold hostage humans and other beings for experimentation.

The Infiltration and Impersonation of Terran Leaders by Malevolent Extraterrestrials

October 27th, 2021

At the time of the last intel drop on October 24, 2021, Val Nek did not want me to yet disclose the Killy Tokurt's connection to the government, specifically the Central Intelligence Agency (CIA). This species, part of the Orion Alliance, are experts in a practice called soul scalping and offered their services to the Central Intelligence Agency and other factions of the Terran government. The Killy Tokurt offered this service to the CIA, who was partnered also with the Ciakahrr Empire, to replace government leaders in positions of power. In other words, this service was to infiltrate the Terran government with extraterrestrial presence and further establish an empire of tyrannical control governing the Terran people. With the completion of the war underground and these bases finally cleared, this is no longer a threat, nor should this ever happen again to the beautiful people of Terra.

As mentioned previously, impersonating Terran leaders is a process that is often done by soul scalping. Removing the light body or soul of an individual and replacing the physical vessel with an extraterrestrial presence using technology.

This process was common to the CIA for the purpose of maintaining control over the government of Terra and specifically the United States. Another practice, but is rarer, is a shapeshifter impersonating a Terran leader. The reason this practice is rarer is because it takes time and energy to hold a shape for an extended period. In other words, for more permanent operations, soul scalping was a more preferred practice of impersonation. There are ways the reptilians shapeshift, and it is done using technology. They have belts, called frequency belts, which are usually black. These belts help stabilize their frequency, the arrangement of molecules in the third density or the chosen density. These shapeshifters require energy to hold a shifted shape and for this reason, soul scalping is preferred. Once the human or Terran soul has been removed from its original physical vessel, it is placed in a little box and lives a simulated reality for an unprecedented amount of time, in other words, unless rescued, the soul is stuck forever, living in a fictitious scenario, like a dream. Often, the person who is a victim to this practice is considered property of the deep state, what we call the cabal, and their personal free will has long been relinquished. Once contracted to work for the corrupt Terran government, they are obligated to oblige by the rules of the institution. To inhabit a Terran vessel, the extraterrestrials install a technology into the brain, specifically the cerebral cortex, where the vessel can be operated remotely. There are several locations where this was done, two of them being Dulce, New Mexico and Area 51 in Nevada. There are operators, you can call them, that operate these vessels remotely. Some are operated above ground in the CIA.

Val Nek: The Federation recovered this information, the last part of the Terran war. You see, we must dismantle their army before we can dismantle their leadership. Once their force was greatly weakened, we recovered the list of Terran leaders that were being impersonated, the list was quite long. High ranking officials in the Federation, including myself, were given this information to execute arrests and recover the Terran vessels. Many of these vessels were operated in the headquarters of the Central Intelligence Agency. Once prepared, the Federation had a duty to invade and dismantle these remote operating systems and remove extraterrestrial control of this government agency.

A Future Without Nuclear Weapons

The United States signed the Greada Treaty in 1954 under the agreement that the military could keep manufacturing and storing nuclear weapons for future use. Dwight Eisenhower's military industrial complex had a thirst for power and domination. Relinquishing control of these weapons of mass destruction and making agreements with the Galactic Federation of Worlds instead, was not appealing. In our future, there will not be nuclear weapons that jeopardize the precious lives of the Terran people and the health of the planet.

> VN: I am happy to report on this. Nuclear weapons are easily dismantled using technology from the Federation. This technology was offered to governments of your people, in the 1950's, but declined. I can now report that this technology is in the hands of the Earth Alliance, and they have graciously accepted our viewpoint of nuclear weapons. Our viewpoint is this: these are weapons of mass destruction, for all involved, and will not be beneficial for planet Terra. This technology, to dismantle nuclear weapons, uses magnetic frequency. The magnetic force is made from elements that are not known to planet Terra. It is rather simple when you think of a bomb as a simple chemical reaction, how to reverse a chemical reaction using elements, is simple technology.

The End of the War

and a Message for the People of Terra

High Commander Ardaana is commander of the Galactic Federation of World's troops in this outpost surrounding Terra. She is a noble woman, one of strength and vigor. As beautiful as she is smart, her strength and courage has led the men and women through the galactic battle on Terra. Now that the Galactic Federation of Worlds has liberated planet Terra from hostile extraterrestrial infiltration, it is the Terran people's responsibility to choose victory and reclaim their power. The Federation has done its duty, to intervene on behalf of the galaxy, but the Terran people must reclaim their sovereignty from their corrupt government. The cabal's power is now only illusion. They have no military allies. The time to liberate ourselves is NOW.

She and Val Nek connected with me to give the people of Terra a final message:

Ardaana: As High Commander of the Galactic Federation of Worlds, I have fought tirelessly, against all peril, alongside my crew and members of the Earth Alliance to liberate your people. We have fought an uphill battle, removing extraterrestrial infiltration from your planet, never wavering from our commitment to what is true. Your people have seen great disaster, as you watched your planet be ravaged and your people's consciousness be suppressed. The time is now to rise as Terrans, for nothing is stopping you and nothing can stop what is coming. The future of your people remains in your hands. Slaves do not free themselves unless they want to, unless they have a cause. The cause is this: for the freedom and sovereignty of every being of life, you must rise to the occasion and claim your freedom. We cannot do it for you, our job here is done. There is no limit to what your people can achieve through one heart, bonded together. Should you choose to claim what is rightfully yours, I repeat again: Nothing can stop what is coming.

The Death of President John F. Kennedy

It is my honor to share with the people of Terra one last truth. President John F Kennedy, who served as president and was murdered long before I was born, shall forever remain a patriot to humanity and the American people. Below I have shared the intel that Val Nek gave me regarding his assassination on November 22, 1963. President Kennedy's Inaugural address of 1961 serves as a perfect ending to this book: "With a good conscience our only sure reward, with history the final judge of our deeds, let us go forth to lead the land we love, asking His blessing and His help, but knowing that here on Earth God's work must truly be our own."-John F. Kennedy

Val Nek: The death of John F. Kennedy was orchestrated by the Central Intelligence Agency, in partnership with the Taal-Shiar. The Taal-Shiar are brown-haired humanoid beings from a planet called Omankhera and now live the Jaha System or Alcyone star system in the Pleiades. They are enemies of the Federation and have worked alongside the cabal and Ciakahrr Empire. John F. Kennedy, I can confirm was working with the Earth Alliance, who secretly partnered with the United States Navy and Galactic Federation of Worlds. Our troops were prepared to draft agreements for disclosure. Agreements that would liberate your people and put an end to the tyranny of the Ciakahrr Empire and Orion Alliance. Of course, our enemies were not pleased and spoiled the plans. I will reference the United States Navy secretly building spacecraft, advanced spacecraft in the 1960's. These constructs were given from the Galactic Federation of Worlds, in hopes to prepare a star fleet and overthrow the tyrannical control on Planet Terra. Unfortunately, the assassination of John F. Kennedy could not be prevented, and plans were re-arranged. We gift you now with the opportunity to take back your planet, to step onto the stage of victory and claim your prize: FREEDOM.

<u>Wise words from President John F. Kennedy's</u>
<u>Inaugural Address, January 20th, 1961:</u>

"We observe today not a victory of party, but a celebration of freedom—symbolizing an end, as well as a beginning—signifying renewal, as well as change. For I have sworn before you and Almighty God the same solemn oath our forebears prescribed nearly a century and three quarters ago.

The world is very different now. For man holds in his mortal hands the power to abolish all forms of human poverty and all forms of human life. And yet the same revolutionary beliefs for which our forebears fought are still at issue around the globe—the belief that the rights of man come not from the generosity of the state, but from the hand of God.

We dare not forget today that we are the heirs of that first revolution. Let the word go forth from this time and place, to friend and foe alike, that the torch has been passed to a new generation of Americans—born in this century, tempered by war, disciplined by a hard and bitter peace, proud of our ancient heritage—and unwilling to witness or permit the slow undoing of those human rights to which this Nation has always been committed, and to which we are committed today at home and around the world.

Let every nation know, whether it wishes us well or ill, that we shall pay any price, bear any burden, meet any hardship, support any friend, oppose any foe, in order to assure the survival and the success of liberty.

This much we pledge—and more.

To those old allies whose cultural and spiritual origins we share, we pledge the loyalty of faithful friends. United, there is little we cannot do in a host of cooperative ventures.

Divided, there is little we can do—for we dare not meet a powerful challenge at odds and split asunder.

To those new States whom we welcome to the ranks of the free, we pledge our word that one form of colonial control shall not have passed away merely to be replaced by a far more iron tyranny. We shall not always expect to find them supporting our view. But we shall always hope to find them strongly supporting their own freedom—and to remember that, in the past, those who foolishly sought power by riding the back of the tiger ended up inside.

To those peoples in the huts and villages across the globe struggling to break the bonds of mass misery, we pledge our best efforts to help them help themselves, for whatever period is required— not because the Communists may be doing it, not because we seek their votes, but because it is right. If a free society cannot help the many who are poor, it cannot save the few who are rich.

To our sister republics south of our border, we offer a special pledge—to convert our good words into good deeds—in a new alliance for progress—to assist free men and free governments in casting off the chains of poverty. But this peaceful revolution of hope cannot become the prey of hostile powers. Let all our neighbors know that we shall join with them to oppose aggression or subversion anywhere in the Americas. And let every other power know that this Hemisphere intends to remain the master of its own house.

To that world assembly of sovereign states, the United Nations, our last best hope in an age where the instruments of war have far outpaced the instruments of peace, we renew our pledge of support—to prevent it from becoming merely a forum for invective—to strengthen its shield of the new and the weak—and to enlarge the area in which its writ may run.

Finally, to those nations who would make themselves our adversary, we offer not a pledge but a request: that both sides begin anew the quest for peace, before the dark powers of destruction unleashed by science engulf all humanity in planned or accidental self-destruction.

We dare not tempt them with weakness. For only when our arms are sufficient beyond doubt can we be certain beyond doubt that they will never be employed.

But neither can two great and powerful groups of nations take comfort from our present course—both sides overburdened by the cost of modern weapons, both rightly alarmed by the steady spread of the deadly atom, yet both racing to alter that uncertain balance of terror that stays the hand of mankind's final war.

So let us begin anew—remembering on both sides that civility is not a sign of weakness, and sincerity is always subject to proof. Let us never negotiate out of fear. But let us never fear to negotiate.

Let both sides explore what problems unite us instead of belaboring those problems which divide us.

Let both sides, for the first time, formulate serious and precise proposals for the inspection and control of arms—and bring the absolute power to destroy other nations under the absolute control of all nations.

Let both sides seek to invoke the wonders of science instead of its terrors. Together let us explore the stars, conquer the deserts, eradicate disease, tap the ocean depths, and encourage the arts and commerce.

Let both sides unite to heed in all corners of the Earth the command of Isaiah—to «undo the heavy burdens ... and to let the oppressed go free.»

And if a beachhead of cooperation may push back the jungle of suspicion, let both sides join in creating a new endeavor, not a new balance of power, but a new world of law, where the strong are just and the weak secure and the peace preserved.

All this will not be finished in the first 100 days. Nor will it be finished in the first 1,000 days, nor in the life of this Administration, nor even perhaps in our lifetime on this planet. But let us begin.

In your hands, my fellow citizens, more than in mine, will rest the final success or failure of our course. Since this country was founded, each generation of Americans has been summoned to give testimony to its national loyalty. The graves of young Americans who answered the call to service surround the globe.

Now the trumpet summons us again—not as a call to bear arms, though arms we need; not as a call to battle, though embattled we are—but a call to bear the burden of a long twilight struggle, year in and year out, «rejoicing in hope, patient in tribulation»—a struggle against the common enemies of man: tyranny, poverty, disease, and war itself.

Can we forge against these enemies a grand and global alliance, North and South, East and West, that can assure a more fruitful life for all mankind? Will you join in that historic effort?

In the long history of the world, only a few generations have been granted the role of defending freedom in its hour of maximum danger. I do not shrink from this responsibility—I welcome it. I do not believe that any of us would exchange places with any other people or any other generation. The energy, the faith, the devotion which we bring to this endeavor will light our country and all who serve it—and the glow from that fire can truly light the world.

And so, my fellow Americans: ask not what your country can do for you—ask what you can do for your country.

My fellow citizens of the world: ask not what America will do for you, but what together we can do for the freedom of man.

Finally, whether you are citizens of America or citizens of the world, ask of us the same high standards of strength and sacrifice which we ask of you. With a good conscience our only sure reward, with history the final judge of our deeds, let us go forth to lead the land we love, asking His blessing and His help, but knowing that here on Earth God's work must truly be our own."

-President John F. Kennedy

Made in United States
Orlando, FL
31 October 2022

24070036R00046